Fragments of Complete Thoughts

Myra Vasquez

BookLeaf Publishing

India | USA | UK

Presentation by *BookLeaf Publishing*

Web: www.bookleafpub.com

E-mail: info@bookleafpub.com

ISBN:

First edition 2022

double exposure

Double exposure,
For all eyes to see
Full disclosure,
You might see hints of duplicity

I will dodge the questions
And I will burn the proof,
But all has been revealed
Everyone knows the truth

Everyone knows when the light
Hits the film, it's too bright
Overexposed

But I kept mine in the dark,
Used the same, over and over
And the pictures came out clear
Perfectly exposed

Double exposure,
For all to see,
Full disclosure,
You're seeing different sides of me.

Double exposure,
You can't unsee,
I don't know what you're thinking,
But do you still love me?

how i love

I always criticize
Myself
For how I love
You
I apologize
For
Not stacking up
To the way
You love
Me

You treat me
Like the queen I'm not
I don't deserve
The royal treatment
But I love
The way you love me,
It's how I wish I saw
Myself

I love you differently,
I love you well -
I love you constantly
And always,
No need for a reason,

I just do

I love you
Even when I'm mad at you
I love you
In everything I say and do
I love you
By letting you
Really see me
I love you
I just do

I'll sing all my songs for you
And save all my art for you
I'll trace the story of me and you
For those who come next
That's how I love you

a best friend

I used to have a best friend
Knew her for a long time
She felt more like a sister
That girl could read my mind

Then we started to drift away
Kind of funny but not that way,
I mean it was strange
To feel the creeping of the waves of change

I used to have a best friend
With the purest of hearts
Now I know her from the distance
Was this all my fault?

Life pulled me away
And I let it
I said I'd never be that way
And I let it
Be that way
And I let it happen
To
Us

cry

Have you ever
Cried so hard
That
You were
Blinded
By the sun?

hurricane

You brought destruction like a hurricane
And you smiled,
It was good for you

You bring the storm wherever you go
And it's good,
Doesn't bother you

But where are you when
We enter a drought,
When we're here begging,
When we need you
Without a doubt?
We could really use some rain right now
I can really stand to have you
Around right now

watching rain fall

Moments of silence are golden,
I seldom wish they were stolen.

Yet when the rain came
And pitter-pattered on the roof
And tapped at my window pane,
I smiled at her music
And let it soak through me.

A cup of coffee in my hands,
A thick blanket wrapped around me,

Watching water ooze
Through grass and dirt,
A welcome drink for this parched earth.

Soothing lullaby,
bring me to sleep,
In silence once again
I find my peace.

a hymn

When I talk to you
It feels so familiar;

When I talk to you
I feel so free.

I can come to you
Knowing
That you know me;

I can say what I feel
without being afraid.

When I look for you
I see a hill
With green grass
Overlooking open fields,
Flowers growing everywhere,
Blue sky,
Sun shining.

I'm looking for you,
I'm looking for you.

I need to

Draw near to you
'Cause it's a wonderful life

But what would it be
If I had turned from the truth?
What would it be
If I had turned away from you?

forgettable

I walk through life
Making and collecting
Memories

All the while
I am becoming
Increasingly forgettable

I know you from years ago,
The classes we took,
Conversations we had,
And of course
I know
When we drifted apart

I carry the memories
And walk around invisibly,
Pretending I had never met you
Knowing that you don't remember me

I wasn't even worth remembering.
What is it about me
That renders me so unmemorable?

I wasn't important in your life,
And you didn't turn out to be important in mine,
So why does it bother me
That you look at me as someone you've
Never known?

glories

Today,
When all the glories
Of yesterday
Mean nothing,
When you can't rest
On your laurels,
When you feel unaccomplished,
When you feel everything was all for naught -

Today,
You remember what you did
But forget why,
You wonder what's the meaning,
You wonder what good it's done for you.

Today is all your yesterdays;
The lessons you've learned
Are living beneath the surface,
Waiting for the right time to shine.

Those glories made you,
But they aren't you.
Those glories are cells of you;
They aren't the world.

You're so much more than those.

Every day
Is a glory day,
No need to yearn
To relive the yesterdays.

life

life
like a room
becomes a mess
clutters easily

life
like a messy room
hard to find what you want

life
like a messy room
takes time to clean up

life
like a messy room
has many chances to improve

life
once the room is clean
you feel a great sense of relief
and you can
move on

my life
is like
a messy room

self-portrait

Glamorous, exciting!
Smart and fascinating!
That's not what I think
When I look at myself

My introspective nature
Has me on an endless adventure
Of self-suspicion,
Finding faults,
Finding imperfections at every fraction

But when I take a step back
And see,
See the big picture
I see that I can have
Some positive qualities

There's some magic,
It isn't all ugly

real

it is difficult to hide reality
you can frame it how you want it
but the real picture will always emerge

blossoms

all winter I wait,
for spring blossoms to flower,
and light up my days.

spiral

My heart is tied up in a knot. A tight know. So
many things are on my mind. My heart is tied
up so tight, compressed in a tiny box in my
chest. I just want to get away. I need an escape.
Things are going mostly fine, but I feel like I'm
always running out of time. I'm hungry, I'm
thirsty, I'm tired. I should be a pancake, but I'm
a crepe, so thin and fragile, a wrong flip and I
tear. I need a break, I need an escape. I need to
sit and let things bake. My heart and my mind
just need to relax. I need to be rescued from this
mass hysteria.

caffeine and candy

I'm on a diet of caffeine and candy, they keep me
going and somewhat happy. Am I better or
worse than a drug addict, or am I the same?
Right now, caffeine and candy are the only
way...the only way to cope with all that
happened, the way to deal with the sadness. All
I want in this world is to erase this madness, but
time has ensured that this will never happen.
Caffeine, candy, and time are my medicine.
Hoping to heal and make better memories. I'm
waiting, I'm hoping for joy to come find me.
The madness will fade, the hurt will erode,
bitterness will fight to remain. I will fight just as
hard, I'm as sweet as pie and to hell with
anything that tries to sour me.

alone

I am encountering an old friend,
a feeling I'm used to knowing,
that is, relearning the art of being alone;
that is, living inside a hole
and feeling normal -
in other words -
being okay when things are not okay
knowing that I will be okay despite what people
say
There's light at the end of the tunnel,
but it's not blinding me today
at least I see a glimmer of hope,
that's all I need.

ingredients

I'm probably considered to be a failure of a woman. I can't cook. I CAN'T COOK. It feels so good to confess it, but it still makes me feel bad to say it. I feel guilty about it. I am ashamed. What do I have to contribute if I can't even feed us?

can...

can someone give us some
    good news,
an update of some sort,
    that there's
new discoveries being made
    and that we're
closer and closer to the
eradication of a disease that
ravages the lives of so many people?

beloved

underneath it all
underneath the petty fights
and the brokenness
underneath all the things
I say and do
that push people away,
I want to be loved
and I want to love
without being rejected.
I want to learn to love
without a fear of rejection
I want to tear down my own walls
but I need help.
I need love.

little me

who are you,
little me?
when did you leave?
when did you change?
why couldn't you stay?
I miss you
I wish I had the courage to be you
again
because little me
was free
and older me
became trapped
in a cage
and even though
the door is unlocked,
couldn't bring herself
to open that door -
still can't
open that door.
but things are changing.
I know that little me is still
here somewhere,
never too far away.